# 10 WAYS TO MAKE IT GREAT!

**Phil Gerbyshak**

# Ordering Additional Copies of the Book

If you'd like to purchase additional copies of this revised edition of 10 Ways to Make It Great!, please contact the author directly by calling 414-640-7445 or emailing makeitgreat@gmail.com and Phil will be happy to order more copies for you. For bulk orders, please allow 2-4 weeks lead time.

You may also order copies of the first edition of 10 Ways to Make It Great! through Amazon.com by going directly to MakeItGreatBook.com.

Printed in the U.S.A. by InstantPublisher.com
ISBN: 978-1-59872-810-1

# Dedication

This book is dedicated to my wife Kim, for all the love and support she gave me during the process of writing a book and changing my life from good to great. I couldn't have done it without you, sweetheart!

# Acknowledgements

Thanks to EVERYONE who gave me feedback on version 1.0 of *10 Ways to Make It Great!* I hope you agree that Version 2.0 is even better.

I also want to say thanks to all the people who read my articles and listen to my podcasts, and especially those who read and comment, trackback, and contact me via email to add to the conversation.

Thanks to Sandy Renshaw for her support and encouragement in creating version 2.0 of this book. Sandy and the team at Purple Wren did an awesome job on the graphics and layout of the new version. Contact Sandy at PurpleWren.com if you need any graphic design help.

Last, but not least, I'd like to thank my LORD and savior, Jesus Christ, because without Your sacrifice, I would be a pile of dust.

*Phil Gerbyshak*
2007

# Foreword to *10 Ways to Make It Great!*

Having worked in the Human Resources field for over 15 years, I have been exposed to many different people and their styles. I have also experienced their "blocks" in this world; the things that keep people from achieving greatness and from reaching their goals. Unfortunately, most people are quite content to just "go through the motions" and let life happen TO them. I have met very few people that make things happen FOR them. Phil Gerbyshak is definitely the latter.

I gained the clarity Phil speaks of after the death of my father. He was a person who had wonderful creative ideas and aspired to do many things; travel the globe, write a book, visit the great art museums of the world. The problem was that he only talked about doing these things. For whatever reason, he never acted upon them and then when he contracted cancer, he found himself at the end of his life with many regrets. I have since created that life list of things to do before I die; I've published a book; I've visited the great art museums of the world; I continue to travel the globe. Some of those things I do for him and some I do for myself.

After reading this book, you will think that Phil's message sounds so simple. There is a good reason for that ... IT IS! Only you can choose how you will react to situations and only you can decide what you want your future to be. If you aren't happy with your current situation, you have a couple of options. The first option is to complain about it and just let it continue. I don't know about you, but that doesn't sound like a good option to me. The second option is to just let it continue and suffer in silence. Again ... not a good option in my opinion. The third option is to change it. Sometimes taking that leap is scary. Trust me ... I've done it many times and it isn't always easy, but it is always worth it. Don't be afraid of failure; it is the basis for a lot of great learning!

The 10 tips in this book outline a great framework for success. Some people just wait for success to find them. I'm sure if you read any books about those in this world we consider very successful, you will find that many sacrificed a great deal or overcame major obstacles; success just didn't happen to them. If you are committed to making changes in how you view the world and your mission in it, you certainly have what it takes to *Make It Great!*

Jackie Valent MSHR, SPHR
Human Resources Executive
Author, *Stinky the Bulldog*

# Contents

*10 Ways to Make It Great!*

# Don't Settle For Nice ...

Life is an active sport. It's one you have to take some control of if you want it to be good, and more control of if you want it to be great. Granted, there are many things that may be out of your control. Early in my life, I realized the only thing I can control is my attitude. Only I can truly *Make It Great!* So I've decided to take it upon myself to always try to be positive, even when things are less than desirable. When you ask me how I'm doing, I am great! Really, I am!

# Make It Great!

*Make It Great!* means it's my choice, which means it's your choice too. Whether you actually have a good day or a not so good day is not the important thing; what's important is how you choose to deal with the things that each day brings. Each encounter presents you with an opportunity to either let it pass by, or tackle it head on and truly *Make It Great!*

# Why Not *Just* "Have a Nice Day?"

*Make It Great!* means I am in charge of, and taking charge of, my actions, and reactions, to my life. I am making it *Great!* If you "have a nice day," you are content to let whatever happens, happen, and you are allowing life to have control over you. Doing so is fine, if you *just* want to have a NICE day! If you're reading this, I'm betting you want to *Make It Great!* This book can help you do that!

## How to Use This Book

Each chapter in this book will have one or more action steps for you to take to *Make It Great!* I recommend you focus on one chapter at a time, think about it, and take the action steps suggested. Write down what kind of difference those actions make in your life.

This book is not meant to be linear, so feel free to jump around to whatever chapter grabs your attention, and come back to the other chapters later. Seize the day, take charge of the opportunities that come your way, and *Make It Great!*

## My Goal with *10 Ways to Make It Great!*

My goal is to pack the rest of this book full of little things you can do to take control of your life and *Make It Great!* If you complete the recommended action steps I suggest at the end of each chapter, you will be making it great!

If you do, I'd love to hear about your success stories. You are welcome to contact me at any time during your personal journey with *10 Ways to Make It Great!* by emailing me at makeitgreat@gmail.com or by stopping by my website at MakeItGreat.org.

Without further ado, let the journey begin!

# Begin at the End and Work Toward Today

### *10 Ways to Make It Great!*

What would you change if you knew you had only one day left to live? Would you spend more time at work, pouring over budget figures, and trying to figure out how you were going to make this quarter's numbers? Would you read just one more email from a complaining co-worker? Would you check your voicemail one last time? What would your obituary say about your life?

If you're like me, I'd bet you wouldn't do anything work-related. In fact, I bet you would see if there was any way to
extend that one day into six months or more, because there is so much you have yet to accomplish. Maybe you would vow to make a difference in your family, with your friends, in your community, or somewhere else in the world. Maybe you'd see if you could skydive, climb Pike's Peak, or snorkel the Great Barrier Reef.

If you knew when the end was, I'd guess you would do all those things you've been meaning to do, but just never had the time to do.

What's stopping you from doing them right now?

Phil Gerbyshak

# Action Step 1:

Write your obituary as though today were your last day. Be honest! Write what you think people will remember most about you.

Some things to include are:
- Who is at the service mourning you?
- What difference did you make in the lives of those at the service?
- How is the world a better place because of what you did?

## Action Step 2:

Take out a pen and paper and make a list of what you'd *like* to be known for if you were to die tomorrow. What's included? What are you doing right now that you need to stop doing? Re-write your obituary now based on what you'd like to be remembered for.

After you have this clarity, think about what you will do to *Make It Great*! on a daily basis, and start doing it *right away*!

## Action Step 3:

What is the one thing you can do to *Make It Great!* right now? Write what that one thing is and a date for when you will take action on that item to *Make It Great!*

**My one thing is:**

**I will do my one thing by:**

*10 Ways to Make It Great!*

# Learn About Yourself as Much as Possible

### 10 Ways to Make It Great!

On my personal journey to *Make It Great!* I have learned a great deal of information about myself. No, not that my favorite color is Carolina blue, or that I enjoy piña coladas and getting caught in the rain. Not those kinds of things.

I have learned many useful things about myself which help me be more energized, and which have allowed me to stop giving away my energy to less productive avenues.

One of the first things I did was take an online assessment called the Clifton StrengthsFinder™, offered by the Gallup organization. The test allows you to discover your five key themes, or areas of personal strength. I discovered that my key themes are:

- **Ideation** – The strength of ideation means I am fascinated by new ideas, especially when I can discover an elegantly simple way to explain why things are the way they are. That's why this book has been such fun for me to write, and is so wonderful for me to share with you.

- **Woo** – Woo stands for Winning Others Over, which means I enjoy meeting new people and getting them to like me.

- **Maximizer** – Maximizer means I enjoy taking something that is already strong, and turning it into something superb. It's why I enjoy learning about myself, especially my strengths, and why I feel it's so critical that you learn as much about yourself as possible. This chapter is all about me helping you maximize your life.

- **Relator** – Interestingly, my relator qualities pulls me close to people I already know. I get a great deal of pleasure and strength from being around my closest friends. Anyone who knows me knows this is true.

- **Strategic** – This strength is what allows me to see patterns where others see only complexity. My strategic strength has been very helpful for me when working in the information technology community, as a teacher, and in the financial sector.

Having the "Woo" strength as so much of my character, I also took an interpersonal communications assessment, so I could understand how I communicate and how I could become a better communicator with others. I learned I am a driver-expressive, which means I like to express myself by using any means necessary, and often will talk more than anyone else in the room. I also learned that I like to be in control of the situation at hand, and about how this part of my nature can determine my effectiveness in communicating well.

Some of the tests available for learning about your interpersonal communication style include: DiSC[i], the Keirsey Temperament Sorter[ii], and the Platinum Rule Behavioral Style Assessment[iii].

Another self-awareness tool that is available, for a small price, is an online Myers Briggs® [iv] test. Taking this test, I found out I am an ENFP (Extraverted Intuitive Feeling Perceiving guy), and that my wife is just the opposite of me.

*10 Ways to Make It Great!*

According to the *MBTI®*, my four quadrants are:

**Extraverted** – I'm outgoing, and enjoy talking with people and get energized by groups of people, and I enjoy energizing others. This trait has served me well as a manager, leader, teacher, and a teammate.

**Intuitive** – I act based on what's in my gut more than sensing to see what might be there. This is helpful for me when I get into unfamiliar territory, when I have no facts to back up my decisions, and must act based on what I "feel" is right.

**Feeling** – I make decisions often based on how people feel, and try to make the best decision for all parties involved.

**Perceiving** – I prefer a more flexible and spontaneous life, and don't get bogged down in the details. It's fun to be this flexible, but it's hard because many people aren't this way and don't understand why I am the way that I am. I see this happen often when I agree to do something before I know all the details, just because I trust the person who asked me or because it "sounds like fun."

Taking these three tests has really helped me understand what makes me tick. These tests have helped guide me to things that deal more with people, and less with process.

The more you know about yourself, the more you can take that knowledge to focus on your strengths and the easier it is to spot those that can help you *Make It Great!* and fill in your weaknesses. Self-knowledge helps you compensate for your weaknesses, and enables you to surround yourself with those that are complementary to you.

It's why diversity of thought is so important. If I had 10 people on my team, just like me, I'd be in trouble. Instead, I hire people who are different from me, and we work together very well.

## Action Step 4:

Complete any of the self-assessments mentioned in the chapter. Note your results, and the reactions to those results, below. Ask your friends, family, and co-workers what they think of your results, and see if they agree.

Remember: you can't be great at everything, so focus on what you **are** great at and use your strengths to *Make It Great!*

## Tests/Assessments I Want to Take:

**Results of my tests:**

**My reactions to my results:**

**Others' reactions to my results:**

# Use the 80/20 Rule as a Key to Your Success

### 10 Ways to Make It Great!

In 1906, Italian economist Vilfredo Pareto[vi] came up with a mathematical principle to describe the distribution of wealth in his country. He found that 20% of the people had 80% of Italy's wealth.

In the late 1940s, a quality management guru by the name of Dr. Joseph Juran[vii] observed a theory of the "vital few" and the "trivial many" and incorrectly attributed this to Pareto, thus the "Pareto Principle" was named and the "80/20 rule" became the common phrase to describe how to be more effective.

**Eighty-twenty (80-20) defined**[viii]:
> A term referring to the Pareto Principle, which was first defined by J. M. Juran in 1950. The principle suggests most effects come from relatively few causes; that is, 80% of the effects come from 20% of the possible causes. "The Vital Few" are the 20% that produce 80% of the outcome. When you *Make It Great!,* you put yourself in position to be one of these "Vital Few" that create 80% of the outcomes.

Focusing on these vital few in your life can make a huge difference in the accomplishments you can make in your life. Everyone is good at a few things, so make your vital few, great.

Let's assume you have a 10-item *To Do* list. If you're honest with yourself, you'll find that there are two things on your list that have more value than the other eight things combined. These are the two things that absolutely must be done for the day, and according to the Pareto Principle, the other 80% on your list can be given to someone else to do, planned for another day, or ignored altogether without minimizing your overall effectiveness.

**18**

By accomplishing these two items, you will do more than you ever thought possible. Chances are these two things are often the hardest things on your list. Some would say that doing something is better than doing nothing. I argue that doing the eight little things is a lot like doing nothing, because they're little things that don't amount to much. Doing the two big things will give you the confidence you need to do even bigger things. Then you'll achieve more, believe in yourself more, thus doing even bigger things, and you will find the effect of creating momentum with consistent effort in the right direction is now in your favor.

Do those difficult, valuable things, and watch your achievements go through the roof. Of course, you can always focus on the trivial few actions and focus on just getting any old thing done to tick off many items on that *To Do* list. This will never really allow you to get ahead.

It's really up to you, and I hope you'll choose to *Make It Great!* and make every effort count by focusing on the "vital few" instead of the "trivial many."

## Action Step 5:

Determine what the **really** important items (the 20%) in your life, family, and career are. Spend more time on these "vital few" things, and less time on everything else (the 80%) and you will *Make It Great!* in no time!

Remember: 80% of your results will come from 20% of your actions. The more time you invest on the 20% that are vitally important, the bigger and better your achievements will be.

**Create Today's *To Do* List?**

**Review your *To Do* list from the previous page**

Write down the two or three things you can do RIGHT NOW that will have the biggest impact on you achieving your goals.

Get started on these items TODAY!

## Never Stop Learning!

## 10 Ways to Make It Great!

"I'll stop learning when I'm dead!" is my motto. There are MANY ways available to learn, and though my list isn't exhaustive, it should be enough to get you started in the right direction.

One of the richest sources for learning available to you, are books. Most adults never read another book – for business or pleasure – after they graduate from high school. Jerrold Jenkins of the Jenkins Group[ix] reports the following shocking statistics:

- 33% of high school graduates will never read another book for the rest of their lives.
- 58% of the total U.S. adult population has never read another book since high school.
- 42% of college graduates will never read another book after college.
- 80% of U.S. families did not buy or read a book last year.
- 70% of U.S. adults have not been in a bookstore in the last five years.
- 57% of new books are not read to completion.

That's a powerful thing to understand: Most adults **never read another book** after they graduate high school, for business or pleasure. Not a single book. How far ahead could you get if you read a book a week, a book a month, or even just a book a year? Reading books can help keep your mind sharp.

The biggest reason given for not reading? "I don't have time!" So how can you possibly fit in the time to read a book a week? The easiest, most painless way to "read" a book a week (or a month) is to listen to them via MP3 or on CD, in your car, or when you exercise.

Where can you get these audio books? These days, almost every book worth reading (this one will be on audio soon too) is on audio CD. You can get audio CDs at your public library, at your local bookseller or at various places online.

"But I don't have time to listen to an MP3 player, or to exercise, and my kids always want me to spend time with them. Then how do I listen to these books?" Easy – you listen to them in your car on your way back and forth to work, to school, to wherever you are going. As Zig Ziglar says, "Your car is your university!" I couldn't agree more.

Here are a few of my favorite non-fiction recommendations to help you get started:

*All Marketers are Liars* – Seth Godin
*Pitch Like a Girl* – Ronna Lichtenberg
*Between Trapezes* – Gail Blanke
*Death By Meeting* – Patrick Lencioni
*First Things First* – Stephen R. Covey
*Today Matters* – John C. Maxwell
*How to Win Friends and Influence People* – Dale Carnegie
*Leadership is an Art* – Max Depree
*Love is the Killer App* – Tim Sanders
*The Art of the Start* – Guy Kawasaki
*The Best Year of Your Life* – Debbie Ford
*The Fred Factor* – Mark Sanborn
*The Power of Positive Thinking* – Norman Vincent Peale
*Think and Grow Rich* – Napoleon Hill

The benefits of lifelong learning are endless. Think of how much further ahead you could be with your life's goals if you read one book a week. If you devoted an hour to reading, you could definitely achieve more, and those extra 20 or more books a year would easily make you an expert on whatever you wanted to be an expert in. Then, once you're an expert, you'll make more money, have more time and be more knowledgeable so you can devote your efforts to those things you really want to do — the 20% that gets you the 80% you need to *Make It Great!*

# Six Tips for Easy Lifelong Learning

Reading or listening to books is just one way to learn. Below are six of my other favorite tips. I've incorporated them all at one point in my life or another, though I don't recommend doing all of them at the same time.

**1. Join a professional organization and use their training outlets** – You may already be part of an organization like Toastmasters, a local writer's workshop group, or something else of that nature. There are a wealth of other organizations out there to suit your interests and needs. If you're not sure, ask around. You'll be surprised to find out which organizations the people around you are affiliated with, and you can find out if the organization is worth your time before you even get started.

Currently I serve in Toastmasters International as an officer, and I've learned great communications, leadership, and time management skills because of my involvement.

Also, I'm involved with HDI (formerly Help Desk Institute) as a local chapter officer. I've attended annual conferences, local chapter training, and presented to my chapter and other chapters, as well as presented at the annual conference. This helps me meet other professionals in my field who can offer me advice and feedback to be the best I can be in my field.

**2. Pursue a degree** – Starting or completing an undergraduate degree can help you *Make It Great!* by increasing your credentials. For some, an advanced degree like an MBA or Master's degree in a particular field may be what's needed to advance your career path or to stay sharp in your current job. There are a number of programs available to you - some are online, some are taught in the traditional classroom setting, and some blend the two. Most schools offer flexible schedules and have offerings to fit into even the busiest schedule.

I completed my bachelor's degree at night, while I was working full-time. It took a little longer, but I appreciate it a lot more than I would have had I not worked so long and hard to earn my degree.

One other thing to keep in mind is that the professors you get for your night school classes generally have much more "real world" experience than the professors who do nothing but teach. This will allow you to learn from experts in their field not only what's in the book but also what they've learned on-the-job.

**3. Get Certified** – An industry-specific certification is required to stay current in many jobs. Often you can pick up a book for self-paced study or take a class online to get the certification to increase your knowledge. Check with your employer, as many companies offer tuition reimbursement for certification programs, and will provide sources for you to choose from.

**4. Take advantage of your company's training offerings** – Many companies offer in-house training to associates. Talk to your manager, supervisor, or HR department about the classes that are available to you. Doing training in what you're already skilled in can help take your skills from very good, to great! Often, companies will pay for training that relates directly to your job, you just have to find the connection.

**5. Visit a website about what you want to learn** –
If you're looking for a good book or a useful website, use a
search engine like Google.com, MSN.com, or Yahoo.com
and enter a few keywords about a topic you want to learn
more about. The Internet is full of information that can help
you learn more about what you need to know.

Many authors and other experts freely give away a sampling
(or more) of their information on their website or on their
blog. Often, they'll share their favorite resources and offer
you some useful links to learn more about the topic. My
website is full of these links and resources, and I encourage
you to visit MakeItGreat.org when you're looking to learn
more about self-improvement and personal development.

An easy way to search for a great blog is to use Google's blog
search (http://blogsearch.google.com) and Technorati
(http://www.technorati.com). Both have their pluses and
minuses, so combining the two searches will ensure you get
the information you need.

**6. Find a mentor** – A mentor is someone who is more
knowledgeable or more experienced than you are in a
particular area. At work, you can look for someone you are
comfortable asking questions. Offer to take them to lunch
and pick their brain.

Another alternative is to look online and email an expert.
You'd be surprised at how many people are willing to help, if
you'll just ask them. Maybe they'll even become a formal
mentor of yours and be willing to invest some of their time in
helping you advance your career and your life.

Don't be shy! Ask *someone* to be your mentor and learn
from someone else's experiences instead of just relying on
your own.

## Action Step 6:

If you don't already have one, go get a library card right now. Pick a topic that will help you make your life and/or your career great, and make it one of your goals to read at least a book a month, every month, for the next year. Some possible topics might include how to write more effectively, ways to improve your written or verbal communication skills, how to understand more about people, the various learning styles, or anything else that you think you need to learn. Repeat this practice each year until you know everything about that topic, then change topics and do it again!

Send an email to makeitgreat@gmail.com if you'd like a personal book recommendation or two.

**Two topics I am interested in are:**




**Books or resources I will use to learn about my top two topics:**

*10 Ways to Make It Great!*

Phil Gerbyshak

# Surround Yourself with Those Who Can Help You

> *"The answer is always no ...*
> *unless you ask."*
> *– Unknown*

If you don't ask someone for help, people can't help you. They won't even know you need help. Most people enjoy helping others. By asking for their help, you're giving them a chance to help you *Make It Great!* and be your hero.

So I say ask away, and do not be concerned if you may never be able to repay their kindness and compassion. Ask anyway, for you can pay it forward and help someone else who may not be able to repay you.

> *"It's not what you know, it's*
> *who you know, that's*
> *important." – Unknown*

I'm sure you've heard this saying a thousand times before, but let me change this slightly to tell you what's important now:

> *"It's not what you know, it's*
> ***who knows you*** *that's*
> *important."*

Remember the key part of this new way of thinking: you may feel you "know" people, but if those people don't "know" you, what kind of relationship is that? How can they help you if they don't know you?

## Surround Yourself with Those Who Help

People love to talk about themselves, and they are more likely to have a positive impression of you if you ask them questions about themselves.

### 10 Ways to Make It Great!

Encourage people to tell you how they're really doing by asking open-ended questions. The next chapter will help you learn more about the power of open-ended questions.

Don't answer others' questions to you with the adjective "fine." Think of "fine" as the acronym "Feelings I'm Not Expressing." Is that really what you're trying to get across to people, that you're hiding your feelings? Be open, be honest, and just let it be!

So get out there, ask questions, and get to know people. Let people get to know you!

**CAUTION:** You just might meet someone you can call your friend!

## Action Step 7:

If you don't have personal business cards, make some on your home computer. A quick and easy business card can be made with a headshot of you on one side of the card, combined with all of your contact information on the other side of the card. Include your personal mantra or favorite quote if you have one, or any other point of interest that might be a conversation starter.

Another option would be to go to an office supply store and order their least expensive cards, or go to an online business card creator like VistaPrint.com and design your own card. When you factor in the cost of ink cartridges, this way may actually be cheaper than printing your own, though if you decide to change designs, you may have more cards than you need.

## Action Step 8:

Now that you have your business cards, use them
frequently and effectively. Put 10 cards in your
pocket every time you leave the house. Put 10 cards
in your car, put 10 in your briefcase or book-bag,
and put three or four in your wallet. You never know
when you're going to get an opportunity to meet
someone who can help you or who you can help.

## Action Step 9:

Join an organization related to your current career, or if you want to make a career switch soon, join an organization that's related to the career you want to be in. Make it a point to attend every meeting for the next six months, and to meet at least three new people at each meeting. Exchange business cards, do breakfast, lunch, dinner or coffee with these new people, and pick their brains about how they got good at their current position, and if they could help you learn more. Most people want to help, you just need to ask!

## Action Step 10:

Think about your three best friends. Find out what's really going on in their life. Don't take "fine" for an answer. Challenge them to *Make It Great!* by sharing their struggles and joys with you. Invest time in them and share your struggles and joys with them after they have shared with you. Together, you can find the answers that can help each of you *Make It Great!*

# Feed Your *Friendlies*

*10 Ways to Make It Great!*

In order to *Make It Great!* you absolutely must make the time to nourish the relationships that give you the most energy, provide you with the most insight, and are the best for you, whenever you can. These *friendlies* are usually folks you know intimately, like family, your best friends, or a co-worker.

You need to know why these people are your friendlies, how you can help them, and how they can help you. How do you find this out?

## Ask Open-Ended Questions

Learning to know more about your friendlies starts by asking a few open-ended questions. An open-ended question is a question that cannot be answered with a simple yes or no. They are open-ended because they offer people the opportunity to tell a story. You never know when you'll get an opportunity to get to know someone more, so always have a few open-ended questions ready to ask.

Below are a few sample open-ended questions:

- Tell me more about (insert whatever someone just mentioned that you have a genuine interest in).
- How did that make you feel?
- Share your greatest joy in life.
- What does that mean to you?
- Tell me about the best vacation you've ever taken.
- What's the best advice you've ever received?

Phil Gerbyshak

# Action Step 11:

Determine who your friendlies are; write your list of names below of those you enjoy spending more time with.

**My Friendlies Are:**

## Action Step 12:

Schedule time with your friendlies, writing down at least five specific dates below over the next six months. Choose a venue and save the date!

# Dream Big Dreams, Do Big Things!

## 10 Ways to Make It Great!

How can dreams help you do more and be more than you ever thought possible? How can you make your dreams a more powerful force in your life?

Let's begin with "How can I make dreams a more powerful part of my life?" The first step is to go to bed thinking about that which you want to dream about. Turn off the TV and turn on something you want to dream about.

For example, if you want to dream about accomplishing more in life, re-read your goals right before you fall asleep. Re-read the goals again when you wake up in the morning. Watch your level of achievement soar!

Having powerful dreams can help you do more and be more than you ever thought possible. The more you think about something, consciously or unconsciously, the more you find ways to accomplish those thoughts.

If your goal is to make $250,000 per year, and you write it down, and re-read it before bed, your mind will automatically think of new ways for you to make more money.

So how can you become a better dreamer? First, set up a *dream room*, a room or a place you can go to get away from it all and just think. This could be outside, under a favorite tree, in your basement, or anywhere that you have the freedom to dream! Stock this place with a notebook, a few pens and pencils, and a music playing device. If you're more auditory, a tape recorder can be used to record your thoughts. No matter where this place is, make it a special place, and go there whenever you need to dream. Make it special, and you'll *Make It Great!*

Phil Gerbyshak

# Dream Big Dreams, Do Big Things!

Take this time to become an expert on a topic that will help make your dreams a reality. I encourage you to go back and re-read Chapter Four, *Never Stop Learning!* for tips on how to do this.

Go to the library and get all the books you can get about the topic and read them. Take them to your dream room with you, and make notes on what you read, and use these to help clarify your goals.

Most importantly, be persistent and patient with yourself. You won't be a great dreamer right away. It will take time, and that's okay. In fact, that's more than okay, that's normal.

## Action Step 13:

Dream a BIG dream. Write it down below. Use descriptive words to make your dream real to you! This book was the result of one of my big dreams! Don't worry what others think about your big dream. You're doing this for YOU and only YOU!

**My first BIG dream is:**

## Action Step 14:

Buy a few magazines, draw a few pictures, or search the Internet for graphics that show your dreams achieved. Create a collage, and hang it somewhere you can see it frequently. Review it frequently to remind yourself of the great things you are going to achieve.

## Action Step 15:

Share your dream with two people you know will support your dreams. Ask them to check in with you in 30 days, 90 days, six months, and every year until your dream is achieved to your satisfaction. This accountability circle is key to achieving your dreams. The more supportive people you have around you, the faster it will become reality.

## Action Step 16:

Repeat action steps 14 and 15 until you've achieved everything you want to achieve in your life.

*10 Ways to Make It Great!*

## Work Hard Now ...
## Or Work Hard Forever!

*10 Ways to Make It Great!*

If I work hard now, I invest whatever time it takes to get my job done effectively and efficiently, and a bit more. Working harder does not mean you spend more time at your current job.

Working hard now means that you must be productive in the 40 hours you do work each week, and squeeze as much out of the hours, minutes and seconds expected of you every day. Give each time period everything you've got, and you will be far more productive than the person who waits 20 years to start working hard.

By working hard now, I am also setting the table for my future successes by investing the time right now to do what I need to do to be successful, to get my name out there so people view me as an advocate for them, and to prove that I am willing to pay the price for success.

The harder I work now, the less hard I'll have to work later. On the other hand, if I choose to be one who just gets by, then I'll have to work hard forever and keep doing "just enough." I'm sure you know plenty of people who do this, and then they wonder why they never get ahead in their career or in their personal life. For me, I prefer to work hard now, put in my time, and rise to the top.

Think about the difference between getting paid for completing a job or responsibility, and contrast that with the job where you only get paid for the hours you work. I enjoy getting paid a wage based on my output, as it drives me on to produce more. With an hourly employee attitude, one can feel less invested in what's going on, because we tend to merely "punch the clock."

**54**                                          Phil Gerbyshak

## Work Hard Now Or Work Hard Forever!

So it's your choice. Work hard now to produce something substantial and be noticed for your work so you can rightfully move into something that rewards you more. Or, work hard forever, punching the clock of life and never finding true fulfillment or rewards in what you do.

## Action Step 17:

Commit to working hard now. Put an extra five hours every week toward making your career great, above and beyond what you do every day!

This doesn't necessarily mean five additional hours "on the job." This could be five hours reading a book or magazine related to your current vocation or future vocation, attending an organization of like-minded individuals, or taking a class on a topic you need to know to take your life to the next level. Repeat this every week for at least a year, and write down the changes you've seen in your life because of this.

# Action Step 18:

Take an hour right now to review the previous action steps you've completed earlier in the book. If you're reading the book first, and you haven't completed any yet, commit to doing at least one this week.

Complete one action step a week, or every two weeks, and note your results below.

**List other actions I will take to work harder now:**

# Recharge Your Batteries

## 10 Ways to Make It Great!

One of the things that so many people neglect as a key with which they can *Make It Great!* is recharging their batteries. They run so hot for so long that they ultimately get burned out. I have been guilty of this, and have stopped just short of completing some of my goals because I started out too fast.

Keeping in mind that life is a marathon, not a sprint can be helpful. You need more than self-affirmations to help you recharge and rejuvenate.

Phil Gerbyshak

## There are Four R's that I've found help me *Make It Great!*

**Rest** – This is one of the hardest things for me to do. I find that I don't need a ton of sleep every single night, but four out of seven nights, I really need my seven to eight hours of sleep to feel completely refreshed and recharged. Your mileage may vary, but seven to eight hours should be enough.

Sometimes I oversleep to try to catch up. These long power snoozes don't help, and in fact, they end up making me more tired than before. I've found that being consistent with getting seven to eight hours of sleep a night is much better for me. You'll find your sweet spot, and once you do, do everything you can to stay in it!

Originally reported in the April 25, 2003 issue of *Psychology Today*[x], it was noted "You cannot make up for lost sleep in only one day." If you didn't get enough sleep for the past week, take the next week or so to go to bed earlier than usual, and get up at your usual time. You'll eventually get back in the groove, but it will take time. The best advice is to not fall behind in the first place.

### 10 Ways to Make It Great!

**Reflect** – Taking the time to reflect on what's happening in my life every few days helps me keep things in perspective and stops negative thoughts before they get out of control. My life is not perfect; I have my bad days too. I make time to think about why they were bad days, and make sure I keep those variables out of my life as much as I can. Of course some days are easier than others. Taking the time to reflect helps me understand how I'm feeling, and why I'm feeling that way. It takes practice and it's definitely worth it!

**Read** – I read as much as I can and examine what I've read and learned often. You don't have to read a novel to get away; find a blog you enjoy, an online newsletter that pumps you up, or just an old email from a friend. Think about the words and really immerse yourself in whatever you're reading. It will help you de-stress and re-charge.

**Relax** – We all relax differently, some by reading, some by reflecting, some by resting, and some by doing something altogether different. Perhaps you have an activity like prayer, meditation or yoga that helps you relax. Or maybe there's a favorite place you can go that immediately calms you down. Whatever or wherever that is, do it or get there NOW and relax.

After you've completed the 4 R's, I encourage you to do one more R: **Re-engage!** Re-engage in your life, and keep making it great!

Phil Gerbyshak

# Action Step 16:

Schedule time for each of the Four R's this month.

**Rest**
The first week, go to bed 30 minutes early. In the morning, write down how you feel below.

## Reflect

The second week, take 15-30 minutes to reflect on how your day went right before you go to bed. Did you get what you wanted done? Do you know what needs to be done to *Make It Great!* tomorrow?

**Read Something**

Pick up a new magazine, newspaper, or journal that you've wanted to read during the third week.

Perform an Internet search on an interesting new topic.

Set a goal to read about this new topic 3-5 times per week for an entire month. Compile the articles you found interesting in a special folder. At the end of the month, review the articles you read and write a page or two about what you found especially interesting, or just note the names and authors of the articles you enjoyed. Continue doing this until you've run out of things that interest you, and then start over at the beginning of your folders. Soon, you'll have your very own library of useful information you can share with family and friends.

## Relax

Fourth is a weekend action step. Saturday and Sunday, set your alarm clock and get up at the same time you do during the week. Make yourself a nice cup of coffee or tea before everyone else is awake and enjoy the moment. Unwind from the week before, and just let the worries of your life go, until the rest of your world comes alive.

## Finish What You Start ...

Some people would argue that the toughest part of any project is getting started. For me, it's often just the opposite, that it's actually hardest to complete something.

Why? Because there's a thrill I get when I start something new. It's exciting to say that I'm starting on a new goal. When I want to get back into the exercise routine, it's exciting for me to buy a new pair of running shoes, a few new t-shirts, some new shorts, and some clean socks. But then I don't exercise, not for very long.

I enjoy the process of setting goals, planning to achieve some great things, but then I fade out and don't achieve them.

For the rest of you:

## ... and Just Get Started!

Thankfully, you're not me. Maybe you have trouble getting started. If you've made it through the book, and still aren't sure where to begin with the action steps and suggestions I've made, I encourage you to just do SOMETHING, ANYTHING, and see what happens naturally. Getting started can be just as hard as finishing for some, so just dive in and do it!

You can do almost anything in the world that you want to, if only you commit yourself to it, practice it perfectly, and continue working on it until you're the best in the world.

# Action Step 17:

Set more goals!

Set **MORE** goals? How will this help you start, or
finish more, as you now have more to start, and
finish, than before? The more goals you set, the more
practice you get setting goals, the more practice
you'll get finishing goals, and the easier it gets to
finish even more goals.

The key is the *type* of goals you set. Set those big
goals for things that scare you, and then break them
up into manageable yearly parts. Then break them
into quarterly parts, and then into monthly parts.
Take it further and break them into weekly parts,
and then into daily parts. Finally identify the tasks
that you can accomplish to get you going in the right
direction. Feel the exhilaration of completing those
tasks and achieving the smaller goals, and watch
them lead to bigger, greater achievements in your
life.

## Action Step 18:

Celebrate in the process of achieving more. As you take steps to achieving your goals, celebrate the milestone accomplishments when you are 20%, 50%, 80%, 90%, and, of course, 100% complete. These are important milestones that when celebrated, can renew your energy and encourage you to persevere through the tough times. Don't be fooled, there will be tough times. But you can make it through!

## Action Step 19:

Time audit your past week so you begin to recognize the successes you had, what you DID get started and what you DID complete, and can analyze the patterns on when you are successful during the week, and compare that to when you aren't.

Next week, do more of what worked, and stop doing what didn't work.

## Action Step 20:

Reward yourself appropriately for your successes. When you start something big, often you think the goal itself is enough of a reward. This is simply not true. Find something that you want and aim for it. The better the reward, the harder you will press. But don't give yourself the prize for 90 percent complete. Finish what you start and get 100 percent complete.

Reward yourself for a job well done, or for achieving a worthwhile goal. For a weight loss goal, you might want to reward yourself with a new suit, a nice pair of shoes, or a nice dinner with a special someone at a restaurant you've wanted to try. For other goals, a new DVD, music CD, or book you've been wanting can be a great reward. Choose something that's meaningful for you and specific enough to your goal so when you see it, you know how and why you achieved it.

Phil Gerbyshak

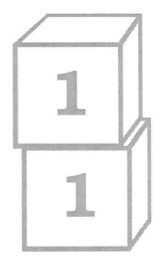

# Go the Extra Mile

**10 Ways to Make It Great!**

> *"It's never crowded along the*
> *extra mile."*
> *– Dr. Wayne Dyer*

You know that there are no shortcuts in life. You know how hard you have to work just to keep pace with your peers. But there is one way that you can outpace your peers consistently, and it's something anyone can do. It's going the extra mile.

Put simply, going the extra mile means you will do what others do to get the job done and then add a little more oomph to make yourself stand out. If the job requires you to do *x,* you're going to do *x + 1,* or more. And that's why you will make it great.

In order to answer the voices in my head, "How can I go the extra mile in my job?" I'll share two ways you can make it great so YOU can go the extra mile.

**1. Know more knowledge** – Take time out of your life to learn more about your job, or about the job you want to hold. With the power of Google, you can do a quick search on whatever job you hold, or whatever job you want to hold. You can find books, websites and other articles that can help you know more, or at least know how others have done it. Use this as a guide. For an even MORE impactful "Know More" lesson, do a Google "blog search" on your topic of choice, and read authentic stories of how others have overcome similar struggles, and if you're interested in learning more, REACH OUT to the author of the article by leaving a comment or sending them an email. Chances are, they will answer your question and help you *Make it Great!*

**2. Know more people** – Grab a piece of paper and a pen. Take five minutes and write down all the people who are doing what you do, better than you do, or people who do

Phil Gerbyshak

what you want to do in your next career, or people who can help you learn more. Go ahead. I'll be here when you're done.

## Action Step 21

OK, so now that you've done the previous 20 action steps, take 30 minutes this week to make at least one phone call or send at least one email to ask for help.

# Action Step 22

If you don't know any of these amazing people's telephone numbers or email addresses, take 30 minutes this week to locate as much information as you can about them, and contact them *next* week.

# Epilogue

Thanks again for joining me on this journey. I hope you've been able to find some new ways to *Make It Great!* for you! If I can ever be of assistance to you or someone you know, please contact me at makeitgreat@gmail.com or stop by my website at MakeItGreat.org and let me know how I can help you!

Until we may meet in person, thank you for choosing to *Make It Great!*

# About Phil Gerbyshak

Phil Gerbyshak's mission on this planet is simple: To help as many people as possible fulfill their goals and dreams, by whatever means necessary.

He believes that each person can **unleash the power within** by improving their attitude, setting goals and changing their way of thinking. His mantra, *Make it Great!* is not just a statement, but a way of life, and he believes it can be everyone's.

That is the gist of *Make It Great!,* and it's what keeps Phil awake at night, dreaming of new ways to help. Means that include public speaking and writing, relationship-building, through professional and community involvements, and from interactions with others and a dedication to learning.

**Speaking**
Phil Gerbyshak is a public speaker who challenges each of us to find our inner greatness. Sharing his message by speaking to many companies and professional organizations, he educates, empowers, and entertains his audience by equipping them with tools, triggers, and targets to turn each day into a *Great!* day!

## Writing

An internationally syndicated writer, Phil is an expert author at EzineArticles.com, contributing author to *Joyful Jubilant Learning Network, 100 Bloggers,* and a writer for the Wisconsin Job Network. His first masterpiece, *10 Ways to Make it Great!,* had its first printing in June of 2006.

Phil has been writing the *Make It Great!* blog since early 2005, sharing over 1,000 articles on building business relationships ("relationship geeking"), management, leadership, customer service, personal empowerment, and personal productivity topics.

Phil also publishes a free weekly newsletter called the *Make It Great! Gazette* and a weekly *Monday Morning Greatness* podcast.

## Building Relationships

Phil tackles complex leadership, management, and customer service issues using his skills as a relationship geek to unearth the best answer to the issue.

Known as "The Relationship Geek," Phil Gerbyshak is already hard at work on his next book*, The Relationship Geek Guidebook*. This new endeavor has an expected publication date of March 2008.

## How Can Phil Help You or Your Organization *Make It Great!*

Hire Phil Gerbyshak to deliver a powerful keynote to your company or organization. Phil has entertained audiences around the United States with his *Make It Great!* message as well as his *How to be a Relationship Geek* presentation.

Phil can also help your team set goals, provide customer service training for associates and managers, and many other training programs. Please contact Phil for details and availability.

PO Box 510854
Milwaukee WI 53202
Phone: 414-640-7445
Email: makeitgreat@gmail.com

## Sneak Preview of Phil's New Book

Tentatively titled "Relationship Geek Guidebook," I'd like to share just a bit of the idea behind the book with you. The book is scheduled for release in early 2008.

## Who is a Relationship Geek?

Anyone can be a Relationship Geek. It's something you learn, though it could be something you are born with. It takes work, but it's worth it! Some examples of Relationship Geeks include:
Dale Carnegie
Scott Ginsberg
Phil Gerbyshak

## What is a Relationship Geek?

A relationship geek is someone passionate about creating and building relationships, by any means necessary. These means include face-to-face contact, handwritten notes and letters, telephone calls, as well as technology tools like voicemail, email, blogs, CRM and other software, podcasts, and the like. This book will discuss all of these methods in a brief overview, and explain how you can make all methods "higher touch" to give them a true personal touch.

# Why Be a Relationship Geek?

"We are one big family of people, trying to make our way through the unfolding puzzle of life. We are all connected to one another in the heart. Connecting with the ultimate source of love is possible through discovering the hidden power in your heart." -Sara Paddison, *Hidden Power of the Heart*

Relationship Geeks connect with people first because it is the right thing to do. People love to be connected with, and finding ways to get deep quick and really understanding them is my passion. We are commanded as people to connect with others, and by connecting with others, we are able to connect with ourselves. We are what we see in others, so the more people we connect with, the more we know ourselves.

# End Notes

# End Notes

[i] http://www.discprofile.com/
[ii] http://keirsey.com/matrix.html
[iii] http://www.platinumrule.com/free-assessment.asp
[iv] http://www.myersbriggs.org/
[v] http://www.myersbriggs.org/my%5Fmbti%5Fpersonality%5Ftype/
mbti%5Fbasics/
[vi] http://en.wikipedia.org/wiki/Pareto_principle /
[vii] http://www.juran.com/
[viii] http://en.wikipedia.org/wiki/80-20_rule
[ix] http://www.jenkinsgroup.com
[x] http://www.psychologytoday.com/articles/pto-20030425-000002.html